HOW TO UNDERSTAND AND *enjoy* THE SCRIPTURES

HOW TO UNDERSTAND AND *enjoy* THE SCRIPTURES

ALLAN K. BURGESS

Deseret Book

Salt Lake City, Utah

To my wife, Jeani,
who loves the scriptures
and has contributed so much
to scripture study
in our family

©1986 Deseret Book Company
All rights reserved
Printed in the United States of America

No part of this book may be reproduced in any
form or by any means without permission in writing
from the publisher, Deseret Book Company,
P.O. Box 30178, Salt Lake City, Utah 84130.

First printing January 1986

Library of Congress Cataloging-in-Publication Data

Burgess, Allan K.
    How to understand and enjoy the Scriptures.

    Bibliography: p.
    Includes index
    1. Bible—Study.   I. Title.
BS600.2.B87   1986   220'.07   85-29212
ISBN 0-87579-030-5

Contents

Preface

As members of The Church of Jesus Christ of Latter-day Saints, all of us know we should study the scriptures and yet the effectiveness of our scripture study seems to be on so many different levels. Some of us read the scriptures but feel they are boring. Others know they should read the scriptures but don't. Many of us like to read the scriptures but don't understand them as well as we would like to, while a few of us just shudder when we hear the words "scripture study." Even still, scattered among the wards and branches throughout the world are people who really enjoy studying the scriptures and are receiving great blessings from their study. This book was written with all of these groups in mind.

Many people desire to get more out of their scripture study but don't really know how to go about it. This book deals with how to study the scriptures, how to establish a consistent study program, and how to come to enjoy scripture study more and receive the many promised blessings and rewards. Much research has been done in order to identify the important ingredients of rewarding scripture study and many examples and ideas from people who are successful in this area have been included.

Chapter One

Why Study the Scriptures

Many people think of scripture study as an obligation that must be met in order to inherit blessings in the next life. They are not aware of the numerous blessings and benefits that scripture study can bring during *this* life. Members of a Sunday School class were asked to read twelve quotations concerning scripture study and identify the blessings that are promised to us during this life if we study the scriptures. The list of blessings they identified follows. (The quotations have been placed in the appendix so you can refer to them if you desire. You may find it worthwhile for your family to make their own list.)

Blessings in this life:

1. increased faith
2. increased desire to do right
3. inspiration
4. understanding
5. answers to problems
6. peace to our hearts
7. new insights

8. greater wisdom
9. closer to God
10. greater spirituality
11. love people more
12. follow counsel better
13. greater satisfaction
14. happiness
15. hope
16. blessings in the home
    a. increased reverence
    b. consideration for others
    c. less contention
    d. increased love and wisdom
    e. children more submissive
    f. pure love of Christ
    g. peace, joy, happiness
17. answers all questions
18. resolves confusion
19. corrects and instructs us
20. increases knowledge
21. strength to resist temptation
22. tells us all things to do
23. heals the wounded soul
24. leads us to do right
25. more powerful effect than anything else
26. exposes snares of the Devil

It is really amazing to realize all of the blessings that God has promised us if we will study the scriptures. Many of these blessings are extremely significant and can give us help that we can receive in no other way. The Lord has assured us that he will always keep his promises if we do our part. He has said such things as "prove me now herewith" (3 Nephi 24:10), "I the Lord am bound when ye do what I say" (D&C 82:10), and "[my] promises which are in them [the scriptures] shall all be fulfilled" (D&C 1:37). The following experiences and quotations illustrate some of the ways that the Lord has kept his promises and blessed those who have approached the scriptures seriously. You are probably acquainted with similar experiences that have taken place in the lives of your family members or friends.

One young man named Richard had rebelled against the teachings of his family and the Church. He would come home drunk, stand at his parents' bedroom door, and laugh at them. When his father had tried everything else he said: "Richard, when you hit rock bottom, turn to the scriptures."

After high school, Richard joined the military. He became heavily involved in drugs and associated with the kind of friends that continued to pull him down. Finally, he became so depressed that he was committed to a mental hospital and confined to a padded cell.

One day he remembered his father's words and asked for a Book of Mormon. He wanted to read it to prove that his father was wrong. Richard was sure that there was no way the Book of Mormon could really help him with his problems. As he read, he marked over one hundred passages that he didn't believe in. In spite of his negative reasons for reading the Book of Mormon, something began to happen to him. He decided to read it again and then again. He read the Book of Mormon seven times, and sometime during his reading, he learned for himself that the Book of Mormon is true.

As his testimony developed, so did the desire and strength to put his life back together. He eventually knelt across the altar in a holy temple of God and was sealed to a wonderful young lady for eternity.[1]

Another young man with similar problems was challenged by his seminary teacher to search the scriptures and take his problems to the Lord. He had no home life, no parents that seemed to care about him. He smoked heavily, used drugs, and was constantly in trouble with the police. As he sat on his bed one night, he was filled with despair. He saw his dusty Bible sitting nearby and remembered the challenge and promises his seminary teacher had made him that morning. He felt a strong urge to give it a try and began reading the Gospel of Matthew. He couldn't put the book down. Peaceful, calm feelings began to enter into his heart. He ended his reading that night determined to read and study the scriptures each night. Since then, he has conquered many of his problems and is now setting a righteous example for his old friends.

These are fairly dramatic examples, but most of the blessings that come from scripture study come quietly and gradually as the following people indicate.

"I cannot speak for others, but I can say that gradually I was transformed. I came to find immense happiness in learning more about God, in receiving his beautiful peace, in receiving the whisperings of the Holy Ghost. The more I read, the more I turned to prayer. Soon I began to feel an intimate relationship with God. I felt support. I felt his patience. . . . Without question, reading the scriptures has changed my life. It is the finest daily habit, besides prayer, that I have ever implemented in my life."[2]

"When I read the scriptures out of the Book of Mormon, it seemed as though my whole day went more smoothly. I was happier with people. My life became cleaner. I would pray night and morning, which was hard to do before. I can control habits easier and ignore social pressures. I really can't explain the feelings I have, but all I know is that I feel closer to God."[3]

Conclusion

The evidence that blessings really do come to those who read and study the scriptures is overwhelming. Thousands of people have taken the Lord at his word and are being blessed for their efforts. The purpose of the next five chapters is to discuss what we can do to more effectively study the scriptures and, therefore, better apply the gospel in our lives.

Chapter Two

Not Read, but Search!

Look at figure one and count as many squares as you can see.

Figure 1

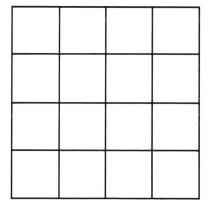

Many people see only sixteen squares and very few iden-tify all thirty of the squares that are in figure 1. In order to find all thirty squares, a person needs to take the time to really search. Figure 2 identifies some of the squares that we may miss unless we take the time to search carefully.

Figure 2

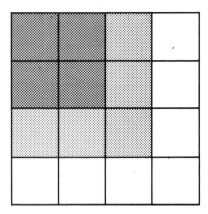

The scriptures are much the same way. As you read the following phrases taken from the scriptures, notice what the Lord is asking us to do.

1. "Search these commandments, for they are true." (D&C 1:37.)

2. "They searched the scriptures, and hearkened no more to the words of this wicked man." (Jacob 7:23.)

3. "Ye should remember to search them diligently, that ye may profit thereby." (Mosiah 1:7.)

4. "A commandment I give unto you that ye search these things diligently." (3 Nephi 23:1.)

Some people do not come to understand the scriptures or receive the promised blessings of the scriptures because they just read them. The Lord has never really asked us to read the scriptures but he has used such words as study, seek, and diligently search. There is a great difference between reading and searching, which is illustrated by the following church history story.

A young six-year-old boy had somehow wandered away from his handcart company during a storm and was lost. When the parents, Robert and Ann Parker, realized their boy was missing, they were frantic. All of the men spent the next two days searching for the lost boy. He was not found, and the decision was made that, because of the approaching winter, the handcart train would need to continue on the next morning.

The father decided to send his wife and other children ahead with their handcart, and he would search back down the trail until he found their son—dead or alive. Ann Parker pinned a bright red shawl around her husband's thin shoulders and told him to wrap their son in it if he were found dead. If the father found their boy *alive,* he was to wave the shawl as a signal as soon as he could be seen by her and the other children.

The handcarts pulled out the next morning with Ann and her children struggling with the heavy load. Robert retraced the miles of trail, calling, searching, and praying for his six-year-old son. He didn't just casually look behind a few trees or leisurely walk back along the trail. He vigorously investigated every thicket, clump of trees, and gully or wash that he came to. After days of desperate searching, he found his son. With the help of God and an old woodsman and the woodsman's wife, his son was still alive. The woodsman had found the boy almost dead from fright and exposure and had nursed him back to health.

You can imagine how happy the father was to find his son still alive and how he anticipated bringing the boy back to his mother and family again. He must have made quick time back up the trail with his precious son.

Meanwhile, the mother had been looking back down the trail for several days. Every minute of sunlight was spent in searching the horizon for a glimpse of her husband and, hopefully, the red shawl. After six days of no sleep and constant searching, she saw a figure in the distance. As she strained her eyes to see more clearly, she saw the sun glint off the red shawl. As a feeling of relief and joy swept over her, she finally gave in to her exhausted body and slumped into unconsciousness upon the trail.[1]

This story illustrates the difference between just looking

and really searching. Too often, we simply browse or skim as we read the scriptures; we find our mind wandering to other concerns. However, if we would search the scriptures with the same vigor that Robert hunted for his son, the scriptures would come alive to us.

One of the biggest mistakes we make when studying the scriptures is to set a goal to read so many pages or chapters a day. Then most of us concentrate on getting through a certain block of scripture instead of taking our time to search the scriptures for greater meaning and application. We hurry much too fast. To illustrate this point, *quickly* read figure 3.

Figure 3

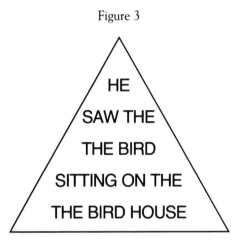

Most of us see *the* only two or three times when we read this statement quickly. As we slow down, we see that the word *the* is used four times. This same concept applies to our scripture study. Many great concepts are lost because we hurry to finish a chapter, a reading assignment, or a book. One page, searched carefully, is usually much more beneficial to us than several chapters read quickly. As a matter of fact, it seems as though the Lord has deliberately inspired the scriptures to be written in such a way that only those who are seriously searching will come to find and understand the truth.

A better goal than reading a certain number of pages or chapters each day might be to read so many minutes each day. You may spend your whole reading time studying, cross-referencing, and looking up the footnotes on only one verse. A time goal exerts no pressure to move quickly through the scriptures. Even the general goal of searching the scriptures every day without any specified time can be a valuable goal. Then, depending on the specific circumstances of each day, we may search the scriptures five minutes or forty-five minutes.

It is not very helpful to search for something unless we know what we are searching for, and this certainly applies to the scriptures. Each time we search the scriptures, we may be looking for different things such as answers to specific questions, solutions to personal problems, insights that will help us present a lesson, or guidance to help us handle our family or church responsibilities.

Many times our desire is simply to know how to live a better life and draw closer to our Father in Heaven. If that is our goal, we should be searching for ways to apply the concepts we are studying as we study the scriptures. Our desire needs to be to *live* more doctrine not just *find* more doctrine. We should give heed to Nephi, who said that he likened all scripture unto him that it might be for his profit and learning (see 1 Nephi 19:23).

One skill that can really help us search the scriptures is that of questioning. We need to learn to ask ourselves meaningful questions as we go through the scriptures. Some general questions that we may ask are:

1. What does this have to do with me?
2. How can I apply this in my life?
3. Why would the Lord ask us to do this?
4. How can I best teach this concept to my family?
5. What can I do to better understand this concept?

There are also other questions we should ask ourselves that deal with the particular verses being searched. Read through D&C 121:34-38 the way you would normally read the scriptures. Please do not ask yourself any questions or read further in this chapter until you have read these verses.

Now that you have read D&C 121:34-38, go back and read it again supplying answers to the following questions:

1. What does it mean to be called?
2. What does it mean to be chosen?
3. Why are many called but few chosen?
4. Have I been called? If so, when?
5. Have I been chosen?
6. How might a person try to control the powers of heaven in an unrighteous way?
7. Do I try to use the priesthood or my church calling to exercise any dominion or compulsion over others?
8. Do I use my call as a parent to exercise any unrighteous dominion or compulsion over my children?
9. What does it mean to kick against the pricks?

Until we understand the answers to these and other questions, we will not fully understand these five verses. Several hours could be spent in studying these few verses of scripture alone. There are footnotes to look up, reference books to turn to, and a lot of thought and discussion that can take place before we may understand the basic messages they contain.

Conclusion

Remember, there is no reason to rush through the scriptures so we can say we have read them. There should be no pressure felt to hurry on to another verse, section, or chapter. The real joy of scripture study comes as we slow down, ask questions, and take the time to really search the scriptures.

Chapter Three

Recognizing and Fulfilling
Our Spiritual Hunger

Many mothers realize that around three or four o'clock in the afternoon, unless they feed their children something, the children begin to get grouchy. The children don't realize that the reason they feel grouchy is because their body needs food, but many smart mothers do. Sometimes young children get so hungry that they actually fight against eating. When this happens, it takes a lot of patience and effort to get some food into them, but after just a few bites they settle right down.

Spiritual hunger, in many ways, is very much like physical hunger. Just as we sometimes fail to connect the symptoms of irritability and impatience with physical hunger, we also sometimes fail to realize that some of our problems may be symptoms of spiritual hunger.

Spiritual hunger is the deep spiritual need that all of us have for Heavenly Father and his gospel. Our spiritual hunger needs feeding just as much as our physical hunger does. Sometimes we do not recognize our spiritual hunger until we have some kind of an awakening experience in our lives. This experience may range from some sort of crisis or disaster to the quiet promptings of the Holy Ghost. The following letter, which was written by a member of the Church to his inactive friend, helps illustrate the problem of having a need and not realizing it.

"Dear Edgar:

"You told me of an experience you once had with a deer-hunting companion in the high Uinta mountains late one fall in bitter cold and stormy weather. Your companion had become lost, panicky, and exhausted from running over the mountainside. He finally lay down under a pine tree, and by sheer luck you came upon him before he froze to death. He was still conscious and could talk to you but in his numbed condition, claimed he was not cold at all. No amount of coaxing on your part could persuade him to get up and move around. He begged to be left alone, insisting he was perfectly comfortable and got angry when you dragged him to his feet and made him move. He really cussed you plenty, you said. You at last, in desperation, picked up a stick and laid one or two across his back until he moved to get out of the reach of it. You had to drive him more than a mile like that, for every time you got sympathetic and eased up with the stick, he'd lie down again. Finally, however, you got him moving faster and faster to get out of the way of the stick and his blood warmed up and began circulating. When he could think clearly again he thanked you, with tears in his eyes, time and time again for using the stick and saving his life.

"I have the feeling since our conversation the other day that you, and hundreds of other good men like you, are in about the same condition spiritually, as your hunting companion was physically." [1]

This man felt comfortable and wanted to be left alone. To do so would have been to let him die. Many times, some of us may be in the same condition spiritually and not realize that we are slowly dying a spiritual death. Some of us that need spiritual help the most may be the very ones who resist it the most. We may not recognize the symptoms of depression, lack of testimony, inability to resist temptation, contention, or dislike for people as signs of spiritual hunger.

One woman, after her seventh baby was born, felt miserable, alone, vulnerable, constantly irritated by her other children. After several months, she finally realized what the cause of her depression was. She said that illness during her pregnancy had changed her habit of getting up early to study and pray. "Oh, I prayed, but never with the same feeling I had after an hour with the scriptures or conference talks. And I felt justified in skipping it—after all, I was so sick. Nevertheless, I had gradually become spiritually weak. Now, after several weeks of having my early morning study, I feel strong and able to care for my family again. I enjoy my children now!"[2] She felt depressed and impatient because she failed to feed her spirit.

All signs of spiritual hunger are not negative. The desires we have to get closer to our Father in Heaven, to learn more about the gospel, and to talk about the gospel with others are positive indications of the inborn hunger for spiritual things that all of us have.

The signs of physical hunger are easy to recognize and include such things as a growling stomach, physical discomfort, weakness, and loss of weight. Recognizing the signs of spiritual hunger is a little more difficult, yet it is the first step in overcoming spiritual hunger. Once we realize that we need to feed ourselves spiritually, the next step is to recognize the food that we need. Elder Boyd K. Packer indicated the right kind of food to satisfy spiritual hunger with the following story:

"In the mountains surrounding this valley there is still very deep snow. The animals, especially the deer, have suffered because of it. They have moved from the foothills to the orchards and gardens trying to find enough nourishment to survive. . . .

"For many years, game wardens bought alfalfa hay and established feed yards in the foothills. The deer came in great numbers to eat the green, leafy hay. The game wardens thought they were doing all they needed to do for the deer. But, as the winter wore on and spring was late, the deer died in great numbers. They died of starvation with their bellies full of hay. This, because nutrients essential to sustain life through a long period of stress were missing from their diet.

"It can be like that with the flocks for whom we are the shepherds. Other stake presidents have thought they were doing all that was needed for their sheep, only to find that some have been *fed* but not *nourished*. Like the deer with their stomachs full of hay, in times of prolonged individual stress they do not survive spiritually.

"The right things, those with true spiritual nourishment, are centered in the scriptures."[3]

Just nibbling at the scriptures will not satisfy our spiritual needs. Just tasting them will not fulfill our spiritual hunger. Nephi taught us how to approach the scriptures when he wrote:

"Wherefore, if ye shall press forward, feasting upon the word of Christ, and endure to the end, behold, thus saith the Father: Ye shall have eternal life." (2 Nephi 31:20.)

"Wherefore, I said unto you, feast upon the words of Christ; for behold, the words of Christ will tell you all things what ye should do." (2 Nephi 32:3.)

An example of a person who feasted on the scriptures was Parley P. Pratt when he first came in contact with the Book of Mormon. He was a sincere truth seeker who wanted to know God's will. He had a spiritual hunger for the truth. He said, "I opened it (the Book of Mormon) with eagerness. . . . I read all day; eating was a burden, I had no desire for food; sleep was a burden when the night came, for I preferred reading to sleep.

"As I read, the spirit of the Lord was upon me, and I knew and comprehended that the book was true. . . . My joy was now full, as it were, and I rejoiced sufficiently to more than pay me for all the sorrows, sacrifices, and toils of my life."[4]

How often we partake of spiritual food is also extremely important. A good question to ask ourselves is, "If we only ate physical food as much as we studied the scriptures, would we: (a) be strong and healthy, (b) have a stomachache, (c) be mighty weak, or (d) be in our grave?"

Just as we need physical food daily, our spirit needs daily nourishment in order to grow stronger. We may feel that reading the scriptures two hours each Sunday is as effective as reading for ten minutes each day. This simply isn't true. Can you imagine what kind of shape our physical bodies would be in if we gorged ourselves each Sunday and went the rest of the week without eating? When we consistently study the scriptures on a daily basis, we accomplish much more than setting aside time only one or two days a week. Elder Howard W. Hunter gave the following counsel concerning how to schedule our scripture study:

"We should not be haphazard in our reading but rather develop a systematic plan for study. There are some who read to a schedule of a number of pages or a set number of chapters each day or week. This may be perfectly justifiable and may be enjoyable if one is reading for pleasure, but it does not constitute meaningful study. It is better to have a set amount of time to give to scriptural study each day than to have a set number of chapters to read. Sometimes we find that the study of a single verse will occupy the whole time.

"Reading habits vary widely. There are rapid readers and slow readers, some who read only small snatches at a time and others who persist without stopping until the book is finished. Those who delve into the scriptural library however, find that to understand requires more than casual reading or perusal—there must be concentrated study. It is certain that one who studies the scriptures every day accomplishes far more than one who devotes considerable time one day and then lets days go by before continuing. Not only should we study each day, but there should be a regular time set aside when we can concentrate without interference. . . .

"Many find that the best time to study is in the morning after a night's rest has cleared the mind of many cares that interrupt thought. Others prefer to study in the quiet hours after the work and worries of the day are over and brushed aside, thus ending the day with a peace and tranquility that comes by communion with the scriptures.

"Perhaps what is more important than the hour of the day is that a regular time be set aside for study. It would be ideal if an hour could be spent each day; but if that much cannot be had, a half hour on a regular basis would result in substantial accomplishment. A quarter of an hour is little time, but it is surprising how much enlightenment and knowledge can be acquired in a subject so meaningful. The important thing is to allow nothing else to ever interfere with our study."[5]

The following questions have been formulated to help us review the ideas discussed in the first three chapters and to help us establish a meaningful reading schedule that is consistent with our individual needs and circumstances. Establishing an effective schedule is the first step in improving scripture study. Consider each question carefully, then write the answers on a separate sheet of paper.

1. Which blessings do I feel I need the most right now from my Heavenly Father?
2. Are there symptoms in my life that may indicate spiritual hunger? If so, what are they?
3. As I study the scriptures, what are some of the things I'm going to be searching for?
4. What will my study schedule be?
   a. I will try to read at the same time every day. The best time for me is:

    b. I will try to read at the same place every day. The best place for me to read is:

    c. I will try to read at least _____ minutes each day.

5. As I study the scriptures, what am I going to do to make sure that I feast upon the scriptures and don't just nibble?

6. What are some specific barriers or problems I will need to overcome in order to make my scripture study more effective? What can I do to overcome each problem?

Conclusion

We need to remember the importance of taking our time and asking questions as we read the scriptures; we need to avoid discouragement. When we were very young and just learning to feed ourselves, we didn't get nearly as much food *in* ourselves as we did *on* ourselves. Now, however, none of us need any instructions to help us feast during Thanksgiving or Christmas. As we continue to seriously study the scriptures, we will soon find that we have also acquired the skills that will allow us to feast upon the scriptures.

Chapter Four

Hearing the Voice of the Lord

There is much more to understanding the scriptures than just consistent study. The scriptures were written under the direction and with the power of the Holy Ghost. In order to understand the scriptures, we must have that same power with us always. The Holy Ghost acts as a special guide and tutor to help us in our study of the scriptures. We should be grateful that we are not expected to completely understand them on our own. The Savior, talking about the scriptures, said:

"These words are not of men nor of man, but of me; wherefore, you shall testify they are of me and not of man; for it is *my voice* which speaketh them unto you; for they are given by my Spirit unto you, *and by my power* you can read them one to another; and save it were by my power you could not have them; wherefore, you can testify that you have *heard my voice, and know my words.*" (D&C 18:34-36; italics added.)

We learn from this inspirational scripture at least two important truths: We can understand the scriptures by the power of the Spirit, and as we come to understand the scrip-

tures we can literally testify that we have heard the Savior's
voice and know his words.

The beautiful message of this scripture was captured by
S. Dilworth Young in the following poem:

Know That I Am!

Youth Speaks:
I do not seek thee, Lord,
In highest hill or
Valley low.
The cloudy sky
Or stars which light the night
Are not thy face
I know.
Thou art the son of God.
I thirst to touch thy garment hem.
To hear thy voice,
And to rejoice in thy
Calm presence, Lord.
A growing youth, I seek
To know thee and to
Hear thy word.

Lord whom ye seek speaks:
My will is in my word:
Written in the rock
With iron pen,
Or graven in the
Gold of ancient plates.
My will is spoken
Unto men
Through prophets.
My voice speaks through
These chosen ones
Who write my words
On the page for all to see.
And reading them—

Given by my power
In the hour
Of their need—
They are my voice
To you,
Young friend,
And reading, you can say
That you have heard my voice
This very day. [1]

As we read the scriptures, the voice of the Lord usually comes to us in one of two ways. The Lord said, "I will tell you in your mind and in your heart, by the Holy Ghost, which shall come upon you. . . . Now, behold, this is the spirit of revelation." (D&C 8:2-3.) One way, then, that the Lord speaks to us is to our minds. When the Lord speaks to our minds, he gives us thoughts and ideas that, if pondered and acted upon, assist us not only in our understanding of the scriptures but in applying that understanding in our lives as well.

As we act upon these thoughts and ideas, problems may be solved, greater understanding may come, or inspired programs may be started or improved upon. Many of these thoughts come so naturally that, if we are not careful, we will take credit for them ourselves. In order to keep this channel of communication open, we cannot afford to do this.

As mentioned in the previous scripture, another way the Lord may speak to us is to our hearts. In the scriptures, our hearts represent our emotions and feelings. When the Lord speaks to our hearts we feel peace, sympathy, love, commitment, and many other feelings. Some common feelings that many people have as the Spirit bears witness to them of the truthfulness of the gospel have been described as "a burning in the bosom, chills up and down the back, or a sort of warm feeling." Many times these feelings from the Holy Ghost are accompanied by tears.

Although the Lord has a constant desire to speak to us through his scriptures, we sometimes don't hear his voice. The following situation will help us better understand what we can do to become more receptive to the Spirit.

Suppose we are at a noisy and crowded airport and spot some of our friends. We can see that they are really excited, and they are yelling something to us. Because they seem so excited, we wonder what they are saying but, because of the noise and the distance, we cannot hear them. What are some of the things we could do to hear them better and come to understand what they are saying?

1. Desire of course has to precede everything else. Unless we really want to hear, we may simply nod our head, wave, and go on our way.

2. We could move closer to our friends.

3. We could try to find a quiet place and eliminate as much noise and distraction as possible.

4. We could put more energy into concentrating and really try to hear what they were saying.

These same four steps are things that we can do as we study to better hear the Spirit of the Lord and, therefore, better understand the scriptures.

Desire

Our first desire should be to have the Holy Ghost with us in our scripture study. This will not only help us to better understand the scriptures but will also help us to apply them in our lives.

Sometimes we do not understand the scriptures because we rely too heavily on our own intellectual abilities or the knowledge of others. Other times we feel that we already understand certain principles, or we have already decided how the Lord wants us to live our lives. We are not, therefore, open to the promptings of the Spirit. Each time we study, we need to ask the Lord to bless us with his Spirit so that we can understand and apply what we are studying.

One nonmember, who eventually joined the Church, said that he had been studying the Book of Mormon consistently for over a year and was still very far from having a testimony of its truthfulness. He said, "I had been searching essentially my own way, rather than the Lord's. I had done a little praying and fasting and was working on the Word of Wisdom, yet I needed something more."

This nonmember asked a missionary for a blessing and returned to his room filled with the Spirit. He picked up his Book of Mormon, confident that the Lord would have him open to a scripture that would help him know which church was true. This did not happen, but instead, the Lord had him open to a scripture that told him how to understand and know the truth of the Book of Mormon. He opened the Book of Mormon and read the following verses:

"Wherefore, now after I have spoken these words, if ye cannot understand them it will be because ye ask not, neither do ye knock; wherefore, ye are not brought into the light, but must perish in the dark. For behold, again I say unto you that if you will enter in by the way, and receive the Holy Ghost, it will show unto you all things what ye should do.

"And now, my beloved brethren, I perceive that ye ponder still in your hearts; and it grieveth me that I must speak concerning this thing. For if ye would hearken unto the Spirit which teacheth a man to pray ye would know that ye must pray; for the evil spirit teacheth not a man to pray, but teacheth him that he must not pray." (Nephi 32:4-5,8.)

This nonmember concluded by saying, "These words struck my heart. They seemed directed right at me. I needed to be told about entering in by the way of the Lord; about receiving the Holy Ghost; and especially about the necessity of prayer. I pondered this message considerably and did my best to apply the principle. Some time later I received my testimony from the Spirit. This passage from Nephi set me on the right path."[2]

After a year of studying the scriptures the wrong way, this man finally learned the importance of including the Spirit in his scripture study. All of us need to desire and ask for the Spirit in order to better hear the voice of the Lord and better understand the scriptures.

Move Closer to the Lord

One way to move closer to the Lord so that we can better hear him is to live more like him. President Marion G. Romney said, "Learning the gospel from the written word, however, is not enough. It must also be lived. As a matter of fact, getting a knowledge of the gospel and living it are interdependent. They go hand in hand. One cannot fully learn the gospel without living it. A knowledge of the gospel comes by degrees: one learns a little, obeys what he learns; learns a little more and obeys that. This cycle continues in an endless round. Such is the pattern by which one can move on to a full knowledge of the gospel."[3]

Find a Quiet Place and Eliminate Noise and Distraction

The voice of the Lord is a still small voice—a whisper. We need to find a place and a time that allow us to relax and really concentrate on our scripture study. It is important to have an inner quietness as well as an outer one. Some of the internal noises that can detract from our study include sin, contention, and the cares of the world such as family problems, work pressures, and so on.

Our study becomes most effective when it becomes a combination of praying, pondering, and studying. Pondering is really a form of informal prayer and many answers and insights can come to us if we will take the time to quietly ponder the things we are studying. The following story illustrates the great help that the combination of prayer and pondering can be in our lives.

Barbara was a woman who owned a successful advertising agency, was happily married, and had three teenagers that she loved a great deal. She was very successful both at work and at home, yet she felt something was missing in her life. She didn't know why, but she felt an emptiness inside. One of her friends gave her some advice that had once changed his life. This friend said, "You're trying to fit God into your life. Five minutes here, ten minutes there. You need to fit your life around God, and you do that with a commitment. An hour a day—now that's commitment. The idea is to take a chunk of time big enough to mean something to you—and then, give that chunk to God."

Barbara first thought the idea was preposterous but finally decided to give it a try. She set her alarm for 5:00 the next morning. When she woke up, it was a dark and very cold February morning but she forced herself out of bed and tiptoed into the living room. She describes what happened next:

"I glanced at my watch and cleared my throat. 'Well, God, here I am. Now what?' I would like to report that God replied immediately, but there was only quiet. As I watched the first tinges of sunrise, I tried to pray but thought instead of my son Andy and the fight we'd had the day before. I thought about a client whose business had hit a rough spot. I thought of inconsequential things.

"Yet gradually my erratic thoughts slowed. My breathing slowed too until I sensed a stillness within me. I grew aware of small sounds—the refrigerator hum, Burt's tail slapping the floor, a frozen branch brushing a window. Then I felt a warm presence of love. I know no other way to describe it. The air, the very place in which I sat, seemed to change, as the ambiance of a house will change when someone you love is home.

"I had been sitting for fifty minutes, but only then did I really begin to pray. And I discovered I wasn't praying with my usual hurried words or my list of 'gimmies.'"

After spending an hour a day in pondering and prayer for six years, Barbara wrote:

"Some mornings, I am quickly filled with the wonder and glory of God. But other mornings, I feel nothing. That's when I remember something else my friend said: 'There will be times when your mind just won't go into God's sanctuary. That's when you spend your hour in God's waiting room. Still, you're there, and God appreciates your struggle to stay there. What's important is the commitment.'

"Because of it, my life is better. Starting my day with an hour of prayer has filled the empty space—to overflowing."[4]

Great blessings will come to us as we learn to better communicate with the Lord through pondering and prayer. These two activities are essential to effective scripture study.

Concentration

The Lord will reward us according to the amount of effort that we put forth in scripture study. The more we concentrate on understanding and applying the scriptures, the more the Lord will bless us with his Spirit.

Reading the scriptures is actually a way to gain personal revelation. As we study, the Lord, through his Spirit, uses a concept or story to teach us what we need to know at that particular time in our lives. This is one reason why several people can prayerfully read the same chapter of scripture and receive different impressions of how to apply it in their lives. Sometimes, a line of scripture seems to almost jump off the page as the Spirit brings it to our attention. The Spirit personalizes the scriptures for each individual reader.

As we work to improve our scripture study, it would be helpful for all of us to ask ourselves the following questions:

1. What things in my life or in my scripture study make it difficult to hear the Lord's voice?

2. What can I do about each of these things so I can better hear the Spirit of the Lord and, therefore, better understand the scriptures?

Conclusion

The power or ability to understand the scriptures comes to us through the Holy Ghost. We usually receive this help from the Holy Ghost through our thoughts and through our feelings (mind and heart).

We become more receptive to the Holy Ghost as we do the following things:

1. Desire to have the Spirit so that we can understand what the Lord wants us to do.

2. Live the gospel better and, therefore, move closer to the Lord.

3. Find a quiet place and time to study and try to eliminate noise and inner distractions.

4. Make prayer and pondering a regular part of our scripture study.

5. Spend a sufficient amount of time and put forth a concentrated effort to understand the scriptures.

Chapter Five

Learning a New Language, the Language of the Scriptures

In the days when the Bible was being translated into English, it was common for men and women to greet each other using the pronouns thy, thine, thee, and thou. As time went on, these formal pronouns continued to be used in poetry and when addressing royalty or other important people. These and other more formal words and phrases used in the scriptures tend to help us feel more reverence for the word of God because they differ from our everyday conversation. Joseph Fielding Smith felt that "members of the Church should be very grateful that the Lord inspired the Prophet Joseph Smith, in the translation of the Book of Mormon, the Doctrine and Covenants, and the Pearl of Great Price to give us these sacred records in the sacred form in which the Bible has come down to us."[1] The scripture language is a sacred language that Church leaders have been inspired to keep from the time of Joseph Smith to the present.

Besides these differences between our present language and the language used in the scriptures, there are other language problems that may make it difficult for some to understand the scriptures. Since the scriptures were first written and/or translated, the meanings of many words and phrases have changed. Our customs today also differ significantly, and we sometimes do not understand particular passages because we don't know the circumstances that led to a certain passage of scripture we may be studying.

In spite of these problems, the language of the scriptures can be mastered and understood and can even add to the reverence and spirituality that we feel as we study. The rest of this chapter deals with some of the things that we can do and use to overcome these language barriers.

Read the Scriptures

By far the most helpful thing we can do to better learn the scripture language is to read the scriptures themselves. Listening to dramatized tapes and reading books about the scriptures will not help us learn the scripture language as effectively as reading the scriptures for ourselves. They can assist us, but we develop an understanding and certain feeling of comfortableness with the scripture language only when we become familiar with it. Our goal should be to develop as much independence as possible in our scripture study.

The importance of independence in scripture study was recently pointed out to a seminary teacher. He found himself in a position where he came in contact with ten to fifteen of his former students within a two or three day period. These students had been out of school for several years and were all involved with the responsibilities of adulthood. He asked each one of them to honestly tell him what he could have done differently, when they were his students, that would have better prepared them for the responsibilities they now faced as adults. Every one of these former students gave the same answer. All of them said they had loved seminary but wished they had learned more about using and understanding the scriptures.

This kind of scripture independence and understanding only comes as we prayerfully read the scriptures themselves on a regular basis. Even though we may not understand everything at first, our comprehension will increase with time just as a child learns to talk or read a little at a time.

Use the LDS Editions of the Scriptures

The basic purpose of the LDS editions of the scriptures is to make the scriptures easier to read and understand. The compilation of these scriptures was guided by such General Authorities as Elders Thomas S. Monson, Boyd K. Packer, Marvin J. Ashton, and Bruce R. McConkie. Using other editions of the scriptures to try to better understand the gospel is comparable to plowing a field by strapping ourselves to the plow instead of using a tractor when we want to increase our production. With all of the helps now available in the LDS editions of the scriptures, other sets of scriptures are greatly outdated. As a matter of fact, many Church leaders have indicated that the LDS editions of the scriptures may very well be the most significant contribution to a better understanding of the gospel that has taken place in this century. As we learn to use the study aids that are contained in these scriptures, the effectiveness of our scripture study will greatly increase. The following is a brief explanation of each of these study aids.

Chapter Headings. The chapter headings in the Bible were written by Elder Bruce R. McConkie. All of the chapter headings in the LDS editions of the scriptures summarize each chapter and emphasize, more than ever before, the doctrinal content of the chapter. These headings are very important in our scripture study because they give us an interpretation and explanation of the text. This can help us to better understand each chapter as we read it. These chapter headings act as short commentaries on the standard works.

In the Doctrine and Covenants, an expanded historical background is given first and is followed by a synopsis of the content of each chapter.

A good example of the assistance these headings can give us is the heading for chapter 29 in the book of Isaiah. The chapter is much easier to understand once the following heading is read. "Nephites shall speak as a voice from the dust—the apostasy, restoration of the gospel, and coming forth of the Book of Mormon are foretold—compare 2 Nephi 27."

Footnotes. A new footnote system was devised that is extremely simple to use. As you read about the different types of footnotes, notice how much help each of them can be in overcoming many of the language problems that have come through translation and through the changing of customs.

1. Cross-references. The new editions now contain cross-references to all of the standard works. This not only assists us in finding added references on the same subject but many of these cross-references clarify and give added perspective to the verses we are studying.

2. JST (Joseph Smith Translation). About six hundred passages are clarified by Joseph Smith. What a help this is in our understanding of the scriptures.

Examples: "Then was Jesus led up of the Spirit into the wilderness to be *tempted of the devil*" is changed to "Then was Jesus led up of the Spirit into the wilderness to be *with God.*" (Matthew 4:1; italics added.)

"Then the devil leaveth him, and, behold, angels came and ministered unto him [Jesus]" is changed to "and *now Jesus knew* that John was cast into prison, *and he sent angels,* and, behold, *they* came and ministered unto him (John)." (Matthew 4:11.)

3. HEB (Hebrew). Most of the Old Testament was written in and translated from the Hebrew language. Many Old Testament terms are clarified by referring back to the original Hebrew.

Examples: Genesis 25:27 reads that "Jacob was a plain man." The HEB footnote indicates that plain, in this case, meant "whole, complete, perfect." This clarification may change the whole concept that we receive of Jacob as we read this verse.

"And the man waxed great" is clarified by the HEB footnote to read "And the man continually increased in wealth until he was very wealthy." (Genesis 27:13.)

4. GR (Greek). The New Testament was written in and translated from the Greek language. Many earlier Greek manuscripts have been found since the translation of the King James Bible. By referring to these earlier manuscripts, we can receive much help in our understanding of the New Testament. Many words that were incorrectly or poorly translated in the King James Bible are clarified in the GR footnotes.

Examples: In Luke 6:19 it states that "the whole multitude sought to touch him: for there went *virtue* out of him, and healed them all." (Italics added.) The GR footnote indicates that the word *virtue*, in this case, means *power*.

"Agree with thine adversary quickly" is clarified by the GR footnote to mean "Quickly have kind thoughts for, or be well disposed toward." (Matthew 5:25.) This simple footnote may change the whole basic concept that we get out of this verse.

5. IE or OR. Modern synonyms and information for obscure or outdated words are given.

Examples: "And in the fourth watch of the night" is clarified by an IE footnote which states that the fourth watch is "between three and six in the morning." (Matthew 14:25.)

Luke 23:50 reads, "And, behold, there was a man named Joseph, a counsellor." The IE footnote indicates that the word *counsellor*, as used here, means that Joseph was a "member of the Sanhedrin, [a] senator."

6. TG (Topical Guide). The topical Guide is a type of concordance that helps locate scriptures on over one thousand topics. This is especially helpful when preparing lessons or researching some gospel principle. It is also very

helpful when we can remember a scripture we have read but do not remember where it is located. Subjects cover a wide range of topics including living water, loaves, locust, judging others, the last judgment, genealogy and temple work, prayer, and the sacrament. References to these subjects are listed from all four of the standard works.

Bible Dictionary. The LDS Bible Dictionary identifies places and people, provides historical background, and explains language and cultural terms. It has 1,285 entries and is 196 pages long. This is the first Bible dictionary prepared by LDS scholars and needs to be referred to often as part of our scripture study.

Example: Under the word *Parables* we are told why the Lord used parables, what the word means, how to interpret parables, how they were grouped by the gospel writers, and which parables are peculiar to each gospel. Our understanding of the New Testament would be greatly enriched by this information on how to interpret parables, and without it we would be at a distinct disadvantage.

If you desire more information on these study aids, the following *Ensign* articles may be helpful.

"Using the New Bible Dictionary in The LDS Edition," June 1982, pp. 47-50.

"Church Publishes First LDS Edition of the Bible," October 1979, pp. 8-18.

"The Church Publishes a New Triple Combination," October 1981, pp. 8-19.

"Using the New LDS Editions of Scriptures as One Book," October 1982, pp. 42-45.

William James Mortimer, who was involved with the printing of the LDS editions of the scriptures, summed up the importance of the use of these scripture aids when he wrote:

"The scriptures have been written, preserved, translated, copied, and published so that people's lives can be changed for the better. All the aids and helps in these new editions were placed there to be used—to bless each person who picks up the books and prayerfully studies them as guides in the quest for eternal life.

"*Now* is the time to use the new Latter-day Saint editions of the scriptures. Treasure your old editions as heirlooms and keepsakes. But study from the new editions of scripture with their marvelous aids and helps. Diligently look to God through their pages as you prepare to live with Him forever."[2]

Use Scripture Commentaries

Many of the customs referred to in the scriptures need to be understood in order to fully understand what is being taught. Although the Bible dictionary is very helpful, much added information can be gained from commentaries. Many LDS commentaries also contain quotations from latter-day Prophets that help us apply the scriptures as well as better understand them.

Until we understand such customs as sowing, shepherds, sheepfolds, Jewish temple ordinances, stoning, and oaths, we will not fully understand the concepts that are associated with these customs.

The following examples of the help commentaries can give us are taken from *The Mortal Messiah,* by Elder Bruce R. McConkie.

Espoused. "Mary was espoused to Joseph, meaning she had made a formal contract of marriage with him that yet had to be completed in a second ceremony before they would commence living together as husband and wife. She was, however, considered by their law to be his wife; the contract could be broken only by a formal 'bill of divorcement,' and any infidelity on her part would be classed as adultery, for which Jehovah had of old decreed death as the penalty."[3]

Circumcision. "'And I will establish a covenant of circumcision with thee,' he had said to Abraham, 'and it shall be my covenant between me and thee, and thy seed after thee, in their generations; that thou mayest know for ever that children are not accountable before me until they are eight years old.' (JST, Genesis 17:11.) Little children are not accountable, but they must be brought up in the nurture and admonition of the Lord, so that when they become accountable, they will continue to walk in his paths and be saved. Circumcision is the token, cut into the flesh so that it can never be removed or forgotten, that their parents have subjected them, in advance and by proxy as it were, to the Abrahamic covenant, the covenant that assures the faithful of eternal increase, of a progeny as numerous as the sands upon the seashore or as the stars in heaven for multitude."[4]

Wisemen. "They knew the King of the Jews had been born, and they knew that a new star was destined to arise and had arisen in connection with that birth. The probability is they were themselves Jews who lived, as millions of Jews then did, in one of the nations to the East. It was the Jews, not the Gentiles, who were acquainted with the scriptures and who were waiting with anxious expectation for the coming of a King."[5]

There are many excellent scripture commentaries available at LDS bookstores. The Church Educational System has produced a commentary on each of the standard works, which are used as student manuals in conjunction with the Gospel Doctrine classes. These commentaries are excellent, inexpensive, and available at Church distribution centers and most LDS bookstores. Two other excellent commentaries are: A *Companion to Your Study of the Doctrine and Covenants,* by Daniel Ludlow and *The Mortal Messiah,* Volumes 1-4, by Bruce R. McConkie.

Mark, Annotate, and Cross-Reference

Since we remember only a small portion of what we read and hear, it can be very helpful to mark and write in our scriptures. If properly done, this will help us find desired

scriptures easier and remind us of important concepts we
have learned previously but may have forgotten.

Here are some basic concepts to consider as we mark, an-
notate, and cross-reference our scriptures.

1. Use a fine point pen or pencil, one that will not bleed
through the pages.

2. Instead of shading in a whole verse or series of verses,
put a bracket around the verse or verses that go together and
circle or underline the key words or concepts. Shading in
the whole scripture makes it difficult to emphasize the important words and concepts. See figure 1 for an example of
bracketing, underlining, and word circling.

Figure 1

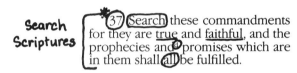

Search
Scriptures
*37 Search these commandments
for they are true and faithful, and the
prophecies and promises which are
in them shall all be fulfilled.

*37- Joseph Smith said:
"No man saved faster
than he gains knowledge."   Rev. 17:17; D and C 58:31; 82:10

3. Write something short in the margin of each under-
lined verse that will help you quickly identify the scripture
when you want to find it again.

4. Information should also be written in the margin that
may add insights and understanding to the scripture. If these
insights come from a scripture commentary or other written
source, write the reference of the source in the margin also.
This will make it possible to quickly support your margin
notes or expand what you have in your margin by returning
to the source. See figure 1 for an example of quoting an out-
side source.

5. If there is not enough room next to the verse to write all you desire to write, place an asterisk (*) by the verse number and write the material elsewhere on the page. Then place another asterisk (*) and the verse number next to your notes. (See figure 1.)

6. If there is a footnote that you feel is helpful, circle the small letter in the verse and the same letter at the bottom of the page. Underline the information in the footnote that you feel is important. The next time you read the verse, you will notice the circled number and realize that there is a helpful footnote at the bottom of the page. This will also keep you from continually looking up footnotes that are less helpful. (See figure 1.)

7. When cross-referencing scriptures, choose a base scripture and list in the margin all the other scriptures to be cross-referenced. Then turn to each of the other scriptures and write the reference of the base scripture in each of their margins. In the future, as you find any of the cross-reference scriptures, it will direct you to the base scripture and the complete list of scriptures. (See figure 2.)

Figure 2

Search Scriptures
1 Ne. 19:23
3 Ne. 23:1

37 Search these commandments for they are true and faithful, and the prophecies and promises which are in them shall all be fulfilled.

Search Scriptures
D+C 1:37

23 And I did read many things unto them which were written in the books of Moses; but that I might more fully persuade them to believe in the Lord their Redeemer I did read unto them that which was written by the prophet Isaiah; for I did liken all scriptures unto us, that it might be for our profit and learning.

*1- Search Scriptures
D+C 1:37

*① And now, behold, I say unto you, that ye ought to search these things. Yea, a commandment I give unto you that ye search these things diligently; for great are the words of Isaiah.

Writing in our scriptures is perfectly acceptable and even desirable under most circumstances. President Spencer W. Kimball once indicated to seminary students that he would like to be able to thumb through their scriptures and see them heavily marked and cross-referenced. The special insights and personal footnotes that we write in our scriptures can be a big aid to us in our future scripture study.

Ponder, Pray, and Seek the Spirit

As discussed in chapter 4, we will never become gospel scholars without the help of the Holy Ghost. We need to so live as to enable the Spirit to enlighten our understanding and emphasize to us those truths that need to be applied in our lives.

This was demonstrated perfectly by a Church member we will refer to as Mark. He had read the scriptures all of his life and had even memorized the Sermon on the Mount word for word. As his home teachers would come to his home they would leave amazed at his ability to quote scripture. He had almost memorized verbatim the four gospels.

The only problem was that he was not living the gospel. He did not attend church, pay his tithing, live the Word of Wisdom, or make an effort to live the gospel. Because of this, he did not have the help of the Holy Ghost in his scripture study. Even though he seemed to be a great scriptorian on the surface, he understood very little of what he had read and memorized.

Just a few years before this man died, he finally put his life in order and became active in the Church. He prepared himself to go to the temple and eventually worked in the temple weekly. One day, he expressed to his bishop how exciting the scriptures had become to him. Before he had memorized them, but now he understood them. This kind of understanding can come only from the Holy Ghost. Spiritual things can be understood only with the help of the Spirit.

Even those with poor reading skills can come to understand the scriptures with the help of the Holy Ghost. This
was demonstrated by one young man who struggled in
school because of his poor reading ability. He was held back
several times and looked like he was headed for scholastic
failure. At age fourteen, he read the Joseph Smith pamphlet
and received a testimony of the Church. With this testimony came a desire to study the scriptures. With the help
of the Spirit, he was able to understand the scriptures and is
now in a position where he teaches motivating scripture
classes to both teenagers and adults.

Another slow reader, Dorothy Kaye Wallace, now an
adult, had been a Church member all of her life, and yet she
had never read any of the standard works. She was a slow
reader and every assignment in school had taken her twice as
long as others to complete. She had started to read the scriptures several times and had always become bogged down
after just a few chapters.

During a stake conference, her stake president challenged the members to read the New Testament. Dorothy
struggled with what seemed to her to be an impossible challenge and finally decided to read the New Testament. Consider the comments of this slow reader who came to understand and love the scriptures in spite of the difficulties the
scripture language posed at first.

"By the end of May—eight and a half months later—I
had read only into the book of Mark. Not a very good rec-
ord, yet something had happened to me. I knew I had to
read the New Testament. I soon found myself 'hooked' on
scripture reading. As the days progressed I began to find real
joy in reading the scriptures.

"I remember the tears that came to my eyes as I read the
beauty of the teachings of Jesus; the sorrow I felt for those
who were bereaved at his death; the empathy I felt for Peter
as he realized he had betrayed Christ; the strength I saw

manifest in Paul as he traveled and was undaunted in the things he knew, felt, and taught.

"Yes, I accomplished my goal. And what a wonderful feeling came to me as I did so! In addition, other beautiful things happened along the way. I found spiritual things to discuss with my children; I showed my husband I could increase my knowledge of the gospel on my own; I found in context the many things I had been taught over the years; I proved I could start, follow through, and finish a task that in the beginning had seemed impossible.

"Best of all, my testimony and love for Jesus Christ increased."[6]

Conclusion

The Lord has not left us alone. He wants us to understand his word and is willing and eager to do his share. He expects us to do our share, which includes reading on a daily basis, using the scripture helps, and seeking help from good commentaries. As we do these things, and strive to live the gospel, we have the right to ask for the help of the Holy Ghost in our scripture study.

Satan's Price Switch

Now that we have discussed things we can do to make our scripture study more rewarding, it is important for us to be aware of a price switch that Satan tries to get all of us to make. In order to better understand this price switch, it is helpful to understand two basic laws. The first law is called the Law of Decreasing Returns and is illustrated in figure 1.

Figure 1

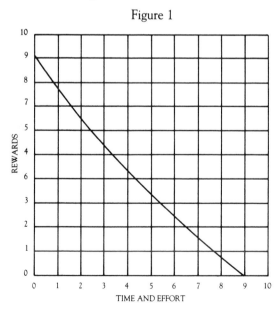

Those things that follow the Law of Decreasing Returns have an immediate reward but the more time and effort that is spent on these things the less rewarding they become.

A seminary teacher recently used marshmallows to demonstrate this law. He asked those in the class who really liked marshmallows to raise their hands. One girl immediately demonstrated her love for marshmallows by waving her arms and yelling, "Me, me, me!"

The teacher had her come to the front of the class and started feeding her marshmallows as fast as she could eat them. She soon proved that she loved them as she proceeded to eat one marshmallow after another at a tremendous rate of speed. After each marshmallow, she was asked to rate it from a high of ten to a low of one, and her ratings were charted on the board. After she had eaten the seventh one, the ratings began to quickly drop and continued to drop until the eighteenth marshmallow, when her ratings reached zero and she reached sickness and fled from the room. Her ratings, that were charted on the board, looked similar to figure 2.

Figure 2

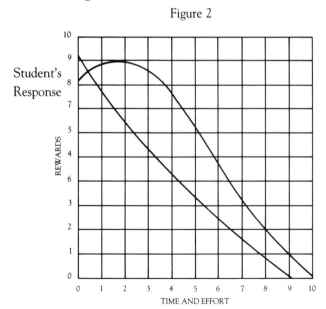

TIME AND EFFORT

As you can see, marshmallow eating follows the Law of Decreasing Returns. This law is also illustrated by the story of two men who went to a restaurant where they were served all the barbecued spareribs they could eat. One of them ordered and ate four full plates of spareribs. As the men left the restaurant, the sparerib eater unknowingly explained the Law of Decreasing Returns perfectly when he said, "You know, the first plate of spareribs tasted out of this world and the second plate was almost as good. But the third order didn't taste very good at all, and the fourth one made me sick."

There are numerous things other than eating that follow the Law of Decreasing Returns, such as hearing the same joke or watching the same movie over and over again.

The second law that is important and helpful to understand is the Law of Increasing Returns. Figure 3 illustrates this law.

Figure 3

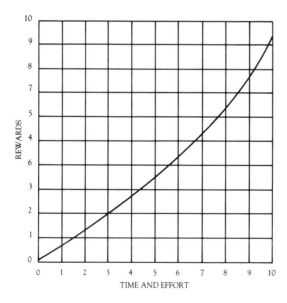

Two teenagers demonstrated their lack of understanding of this law when they decided they would work out with weights and develop their muscles. One of them had just received a set of barbells for Christmas so the two boys met at his house the following Saturday morning. To start their muscle-building program, they placed as much weight on the barbell as they could lift and worked out for three or four hours. They would lift the barbells as many times as possible, rest, and do the same thing again. It was a lot of work, but both of them could imagine how they were going to look with massive chests and bulging biceps.

By Monday morning, neither of the young men could dress themselves, let alone walk without extreme pain and effort. It took two weeks before they were able to move like humans instead of rusty robots. That was the beginning and the end of their weight-building program.

Like many other worthwhile activities, physical conditioning follows the Law of Increasing Returns. These activities may not seem too rewarding at the start, but the reward grows as time and effort are invested. Other activities that follow this law are playing a musical instrument, improving in a sport, developing occupational and other skills, gaining knowledge, and developing friendships.

The reason we have discussed these two laws, and what they have to do with the scriptures will soon become apparent, but first let's summarize these two laws.

Law of Decreasing Returns

1. There may be a large immediate reward, but little or no future reward.

2. The more time and effort spent, the less the reward.

3. The activities that follow this law usually include all types of pleasure seeking such as eating.

Law of Increasing Returns

1. There is usually a small immediate reward, but great future reward.

2. The more time and effort spent, the greater the reward.

3. The activities that follow this law include the development of all kinds of skills, knowledge, personal relationships, and so forth.

As you think about these two laws it is not difficult to see that scripture study best fits under the Law of Increasing Returns. Sometimes, if we are not careful, we approach scripture study like the two young men approached muscle building. We feel that we can have a crash course and receive the blessings quickly. We are disappointed when we read the scriptures five straight days and don't notice any difference. People that play the piano know that it took some unexciting practice sessions before many of the blessings of playing the piano began to come to them. Although some blessings of scripture study may come almost immediately, it takes time and effort to receive many of the blessings discussed in chapter 1. Because many good people do not realize this, they read the scriptures for a short period of time, say they are not very rewarding, or even boring, and quit studying. They fail to reap the promised blessings because they become discouraged too soon. Notice the emphasis on time (patience) and effort (diligence) in the following quote from the Book of Mormon.

"Because of your diligence and your faith and your patience with the word in nourishing it, that it may take root in you, behold, by and by ye shall pluck the fruit thereof, which is most precious, which is sweet above all that is sweet, and which is white above all that is white, yea, and pure above all that is pure; and ye shall feast upon this fruit even until ye are filled, that ye hunger not, neither shall ye thirst." (Alma 32:42.) (For other quotations that emphasize the importance of time and effort, see the appendix, part II.)

With this understanding of the Laws of Increasing and Decreasing Returns, we are now in a better position to understand a price switch that Satan encourages us to make. He wants us to spend most of our time and effort in purchasing those things of least worth. Things that are only temporary and of no lasting value.

Most of the things that really matter in life, including scripture study, follow the Law of Increasing Returns. Satan really doesn't have to get us to commit serious sins in order for us to lose our eternal blessings. He just needs to get us to spend our allotted time and effort on this earth doing things of little or no eternal value. Satan does this one of two ways. He either emphasizes immediate pleasure instead of long-range consequences, or he suggests that the effort required in doing meaningful activities is not worth it and encourages us to look at the present instead of the future. One reason many of us don't study the scriptures more is illustrated very well in figure 4.

Figure 4

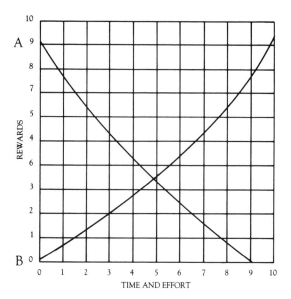

Notice the gap between A and B. Let's have A represent a television show that we really like and B represent scripture study with all of its blessings. The television show will bring us a quick, immediate reward and Satan's plan is to help us think only of the moment. Because scripture study usually takes more time and effort before it rewards us, thousands of people choose to watch television instead. Nephi and Jacob warned their people about this price switch over twenty-five hundred years ago.

"Wherefore, *do not spend money for that which is of no worth, nor your labor for that which cannot satisfy.* Hearken diligently unto me, and remember the words which I have spoken; and come unto the Holy One of Israel, and *feast upon that which perisheth* not, neither can be corrupted, and let your soul delight in fatness." (2 Nephi 9:51; italics added.)

Satan is a master of temptation and works hard to get us to mistake pleasures (TV, movies, sports) for real happiness (peace, faith, wisdom, eternal life). James E. Talmage expressed the expertise of Satan in the counterfeiting of pleasures for real joy when he wrote:

"The present is an age of pleasure-seeking, and men are losing their sanity in the mad rush for sensations that do but excite, and disappoint. In this day of counterfeits, adulterations, and base imitations, the devil is busier than he has ever been in the course of human history, in the manufacture of pleasures, both old and new; and these he offers for sale in most attractive fashion, falsely labeled, *Happiness.* In this soul-destroying craft he is without a peer; he has had centuries of experience and practice, and by his skill he controls the market. He has learned the tricks of the trade, and knows well how to catch the eye and arouse the desire of his customers. He puts up the stuff in bright-colored packages, tied with tinsel string and tassel; and crowds flock to his bargain counters, hustling and crushing one another in their frenzy to buy."[1]

Conclusion

Once we are aware of this deception and understand the Laws of Increasing and Decreasing Returns, we are in a position to counteract Satan's influence and use our time to purchase things of eternal value. This, of course, would include setting apart some time each day for a concentrated study of the scriptures. The following quote from the LDS film *Man's Search For Happiness* summarizes the importance of doing those things, including scripture study, that lead to future blessings and happiness.

"Life offers you two precious gifts: One is time, the other, freedom of choice. The freedom to buy with your time what you will. You are free to exchange your allotment of time for thrills. You may trade it for greed. You may purchase with it vanity. You may spend your time in pursuing material things. Yours is the freedom to choose, but these are no bargains for in them you find no lasting satisfaction.

"Every day, every hour, every minute of your span of mortal years must be accounted for, and it is in this life that you walk by faith and prove yourself able to choose good over evil, right over wrong, enduring happiness over mere amusement and your eternal reward will be according to your choosing."

Chapter Seven

Family Scripture Study

The Church recently completed a study among young men between the ages of twelve and eighteen that indicated how important scripture study in the home really is. The study attempted to determine what factors have the greatest influence upon the worthiness of a young man to receive the Melchizedek Priesthood, serve a mission, and marry in the temple.

The study considered the importance of public and private religious behavior in the lives of young men. Public religious performance is participation in meetings and activities. Private religious behavior deals with experiences not measured on correlated reports, such as personal scripture study and private prayer.

The study found that the most powerful factors in helping young men make correct decisions in their lives were a home life that includes regular family prayer, regular family study of the gospel and the scriptures, and agreement on basic values. It was also found that private religious behavior was very important, such as personal prayer and personal study of the scriptures. [1]

This importance that parents play in teaching the scriptures to their children was once referred to by Elder Matthew Cowley. He was asked to fill in for another General Authority and speak at General Conference on the very morning of conference. He gave a masterful sermon on the Book of Mormon and closed with a powerful testimony. Following the meeting, Sister Belle Spafford asked Elder Cowley how he could give such a powerful address with so little time to prepare. His answer teaches us the important role that parents play in family scripture study. He said, "What do you mean by little time in which to prepare? I had plenty of time. I have had a lifetime. My preparation for that address began when I was a little boy at my mother's knee."[2]

We are all faced with a shortage of time. We have to decide what our priorities will be. The sad thing is that many of us crowd out the things that matter most with things of lesser value. Based on the Church study quoted previously, scripture study in our homes should become one of our top priorities.

Establishing scripture study in our homes is really a three-step process. The first step is to establish our own personal scripture study. It is difficult to teach our children the gospel if we do not know it, and it's hard to teach our children to love the scriptures unless we understand and love them ourselves. The second step is to establish some kind of scripture teaching and reading program in our families. And the third step is to encourage our children to study the scriptures on their own. The first six chapters dealt with step one, now we will spend some time discussing steps two and three.

Family Scripture Study

How we organize our family scripture study will be determined by the ages of our children and our unique family circumstances. The important thing is to establish a regular study program that will benefit each family member. The following are some ideas and suggestions that have been used successfully.

1. Study together just before or after breakfast or supper each day.

2. Base your Sunday discussions or family home evening lessons around the scriptures.

3. At breakfast or supper have each member of the family read one verse of scripture and discuss what was read during the meal.

4. Make each scripture study session as enjoyable as possible.

5. Make sure every child has a set of scriptures even if they are nonreaders. Inexpensive copies can be used and even young children like to mark in their own scriptures as you mark yours.

6. Start with the most interesting stories in the scriptures. It may not be a good idea to just go through each book from beginning to end. This will come as the children get older.

7. Select the most pressing problems relating to your family and search the scriptures together for answers to those problems.

8. Have a prayer before or after studying the scriptures so your children will associate the two together.

9. When teaching younger children, use pictures or some other visual aid if possible.

10. Mix storytelling and reading together. Tell the story and have each family member turn to certain key scriptures when appropriate.

11. Bear your testimony and share your good feelings about the scriptures often. Share positive ways that the scriptures bless you on a continual basis.

12. Try to involve each child by having him hold a picture, answer a question, and so on.

13. Help your children memorize important scriptures and quote them during family scripture study.

14. A member of the family could read a scripture before family prayer. If your children are old enough, they could be assigned to choose special scriptures for this occasion and take turns sharing them.

15. Young children could be furnished with a notebook and pencil or crayon. At the end of each scripture study session, they could draw a picture in their notebook about that scripture reading. The notebook could be used over and over again to review past scriptures discussed.

16. The concepts taught in chapters 1-6 could be taught to your children as part of your scripture study program.

Children's Personal Scripture Study

This step is the most difficult one to initiate, and yet it is by far the most important one. As our children start to study the scriptures on their own, they will begin to reap the great blessings of scripture study. Here are a few suggestions for encouraging them in this important area.

1. Start while they are young to read scripture books to them. Make their story just before bed one from a scripture book.

2. As they get a little older, read with them from the scriptures themselves.

3. Have a club as a family and keep track on a special chart of how many days each person reads the scriptures without missing. Emphasize time (for example, ten minutes) and not chapters. Make sure the names of all family members are on the chart (including parents).

4. Give some kind of reward for every twenty-five consecutive days read.

5. Make sure the children see you regularly reading the scriptures.

6. Teach them to mark their scriptures and make sure each child has a personal set and a red pencil or pen.

7. Encourage family members to mark the scriptures as

they do their personal reading each day and have them share their favorite scriptures during family home evening each week.

8. Ask your teenagers some questions that nonmembers might ask them. Have them try to find the answers in their scriptures before the next home evening or scripture study session. Do this often.

9. Assign each child a person in the scriptures and have them become the family expert on that person.

10. Tell the children that if they are ready for bed on time, they can stay up fifteen minutes late and read the scriptures. Younger children feel great about this.

Conclusion

As parents, we sometimes do not totally realize the great power of the written word of God. One family had a son that just would not fast. He turned eight, nine, ten, eleven, and twelve and still would not fast more than a few hours. Each fast day he would say that he didn't see why he should fast, and each fast day his parents would try to explain it to him. This went on for five years until, one fast Sunday, the father decided to use the scriptures. He sat down with his son and had him read two scriptures from the standard works. The scriptures didn't deal with fast day at all but with obedience and the great knowledge of God compared to our own knowledge. That was about five years ago and that young man has fasted every fast Sunday since that day.

There is a power that accompanies the scriptures that cannot be duplicated in any other way. We need to do everything we can do as parents to make that power an important ingredient in the lives of our children.

Chapter Eight

Blessing the Lives of Others

Elder Sterling W. Sill taught that even though becoming a son of perdition and murder are the most serious sins that can be committed, they only affect a relatively few members of the Church. Elder Sill felt that the sins that are the most serious are really the ones that keep the most people from going to the celestial kingdom. He taught that one of these serious sins is ignorance and that ignorance is particularly dangerous because it is usually regarded as a "little sin." Elder Sill felt that ignorance, indecision, and indifference caused more people to lose their exaltation in the celestial kingdom than all of the other sins combined.[1]

Ignorance not only stands between us and many blessings but, many times, prohibits us from blessing the lives of others as well. This is illustrated by the following story as told by Elder LeGrand Richards:

"Some time back one of our Mormon girls was married and went East to live. When her neighbors found that she was a member of the Mormon Church, they all wanted to know what the Mormons believe. She wrote to an editor of the *Deseret News* and said, 'Please write and tell me what we believe. I know that the first two principles are that you should not use tea or coffee or play cards. . . .'

"We have to have something more than that to offer if we expect to convert them. . . . Every Latter-day Saint ought to aspire to be able to give a reason for the hope that is in him, so that we can intelligently tell why we are members of the Church and not just that we do not use tea or coffee or play cards."[2]

Sometimes, as we serve in the Church, it is easy to get caught up in the meetings, programs, procedures, and policies and forget the importance of setting aside time to study the scriptures. Elder Bruce R. McConkie indicated that it is almost a universal tendency for most Church leaders to get so involved in the operation of the Church that they omit the more important area of Church leadership, which is studying, understanding, and applying the scriptures. Elder McConkie went on to teach that "however talented men may be in administrative matters; however eloquent they may be in expressing their views; however learned they may be in worldly things, they will be denied the sweet whisperings of the Spirit that might have been theirs unless they pay the price of studying, pondering, and praying about the scriptures."[3]

Elder Boyd K. Packer has said that principles of the gospel underlie every phase of Church administration and that these principles are not found in the handbooks but in the scriptures. He went on to say that leaders need the spiritual guidance found in the scriptures in order to please the Lord. He then pointed to another important reason for Church leaders to understand the scriptures when he gave the following warning:

"We live in a day of great opposition, not just in the United States, but worldwide. It grows by day and by night all across the world. Enemies from without, reinforced by apostates from within, challenge the faith of the rank and file members of the Church. It is not the programs of the Church they challenge. They are, in fact, quite complimentary of them. It is the doctrines they focus on. It's the doctrines they attack, and we notice that many leaders seem to be at a loss as to how to answer doctrinal questions. I've had something to do in the public communications program, and daily calls come from all over: 'Help. What do we do? They are challenging the doctrines.' If our members are ignorant of the doctrines, we are in danger, notwithstanding efficient programs and buildings."[4]

There are numerous examples that demonstrate that the better we understand the gospel, the more effectively we can bless the lives of others.

One Church member was called to the home of a neighbor who was suffering from severe depression. As they talked, the neighbor said that she was petrified of all the bad events that would take place in the last days preceding the Second Coming of Christ. Because this good member had paid the price of consistent study, he was able to turn to numerous scriptures that talked about the peace and safety and refuge that would be offered to the faithful saints. As this lady read these scriptures and heard them explained to her by her neighbor, the Holy Ghost entered her heart and brought her a sense of peace and rest that she hadn't felt for several months. During the next few weeks her depression lifted, and she once again became a happy and productive member of the Church.

Another good sister wouldn't forgive herself of a moral sin that she had committed over fifty years before until a Church leader read with her the many scriptures that tell how the Lord will forgive and "remember it no more." This lady called the Church leader a week later and said that she had been able to peacefully fall asleep at night for the first time in over fifty years.

Not only is it important to understand gospel concepts but, at times, it is helpful to know chapter and verse. A bishop was called over to a nonmember's home because the non-member's wife was dying. The nonmember was a lay minister and wanted the bishop to perform the last rites for his dying wife to make certain she was forgiven of her sins. The bishop told him that the LDS Church does not believe in last rites for the forgiveness of sins, and the minister wanted to know why. Using the minister's Bible, they discussed the New Testament scriptures together. The bishop shared several scriptures with the minister concerning forgiveness, works versus faith, and other appropriate concepts. The bishop then knelt down with the minister, at the woman's bedside, and offered a beautiful and inspired prayer in behalf of the minister and his wife.

Because of the personal preparation of the bishop, not only did this couple receive comfort in a time of need, but the minister ended up joining the Church and, in time, doing the temple work for his wife.

As bishops, Relief Society presidents, and other Church leaders, we have many opportunities to counsel others. It is very important to understand the gospel so we can counsel correctly. When we know the gospel, the Holy Ghost can bring to our remembrance the scriptures and gospel concepts that will guide us as we help those seeking counsel.

Teachers also have a great responsibility in the Church. As a bishop, I found myself striving to solve several problems that had been caused by teachers giving incorrect information in their lessons. These problems ranged from Junior Sunday School ages through teenage and adult classes.

On the other hand, as I interviewed ward members, I found many people whose lives had been affected for the better because of excellent teachers who had prepared themselves and taught with the Spirit.

When I was growing up, I had some fine teachers, but occasionally I was taught some things in Primary and Sunday School that were incorrect. What worries me is that I still hear these same things being taught today. One solution to this problem is to study the source before each lesson is given. Too many times, with a well-known subject such as David and Goliath, we feel we know the story and don't actually turn to the scriptures. We then continue to pass on incorrect concepts that have been taught to us. For example, in the story of David and Goliath, it is often taught that David tried on Saul's armour but did not want to use it, because it was too heavy or large or bulky. This simply is not true. First Samuel 17:39 indicates that David did not wear the armour because he had not proved it. He didn't know how to use it, so he turned to something familiar—his sling and stones. Although this difference may seem unimportant, many great concepts can be taught with the idea that we need to become familiar with something before we can use it properly, and we owe it to our students to teach them the truth. This can be done only if we read the source before we go into the classroom.

Confidence is lost, not only in the teacher, but sometimes in the Church, when different teachers give opposing information. We need to verify what we have been taught before teaching it to others.

Probably more teaching is done informally than in any other way. Very seldom do nonmembers seek out Church leaders for answers, but they usually go to their neighbors or members that they work with. Most members who have personal gospel questions or concerns usually seek out a friend to share their feelings with. Even students with problems or questions tend to talk to their teachers after class or some other time in an informal way.

The only way to prepare for these numerous teaching opportunities that all of us have is to study on a regular basis and then ask the Lord to help us when these situations arise. Much harm can take place if we give incorrect information, but much help and direction can be given if we are prepared and have the Spirit to guide us. If we do not know the answer, the best thing to do is just say so and not speculate as to what the answer might be. We can then look up the answer, if there is one, and get back to the person. Another caution to keep in mind is that we can help others understand the principles of the gospel, but they have the responsibility to decide how to apply these principles in their lives.

President McKay had a formula for helping other people. It was simply:

1. Get the information yourself.
2. Make the information part of your life.
3. Then get the information into the lives of others.

Conclusion

As we continue to study the scriptures, the blessings mentioned in chapter 1 will not only become part of our own lives but will naturally overflow into the lives of others. We need to follow the simple counsel of President Kimball and "do it!" We need to make whatever adjustments are necessary to include daily scripture study in our lives, and we need to make these adjustments now. As we do, our lives will become richer, happier, and more successful, and our families and those we meet will also reap the benefits of our dedication and diligence.

Appendix

I. The following quotes help identify the scripture study blessings promised during this life.

Bruce R. McConkie

"I think that people who study the scriptures get a dimension to their life that nobody else gets and that can't be gained in any other way except by studying the scriptures. There's an increase in faith and a desire to do what's right and a feeling of inspiration and understanding that comes to people who study the gospel—meaning particularly the standard works—and who ponder the principles, that can't come in any other way." (*Church News*, January 24, 1976, p. 4.)

Spencer W. Kimball

"The years have taught me that if we will energetically pursue this worthy personal goal [of scripture study] in a determined and conscientious manner, we shall indeed find answers to our problems and peace in our hearts. We shall experience the Holy Ghost broadening our understanding,

find new insights, witness an unfolding pattern of all scripture; and the doctrines of the Lord shall come to have more
meaning to us than we ever thought possible. As a conse-
quence, we shall have greater wisdom with which to guide
ourselves and our families, so that we may serve as a light
and source of strength to our nonmember friends with whom
we have an obligation to share the gospel." (*The Teachings of
Spencer W. Kimball* [Salt Lake City: Bookcraft Inc., 1982],
p. 135.)

Spencer W. Kimball

"I find that when I get casual in my relationships with di-
vinity and when it seems that no divine ear is listening and
no divine voice is speaking, that I am far, far away. If I im-
merse myself in the scriptures the distance narrows and the
spirituality returns. I find myself loving more intensely those
whom I must love with all my heart and mind and strength,
and loving them more, I find it easier to abide their counsel." (*The Teachings of Spencer W. Kimball* [Salt Lake City:
Bookcraft, Inc., 1982], p. 135.)

Bruce R. McConkie

"By regular, systematic study of the standard works we
can go a long way toward keeping in a course that will please
the Lord and further our own eternal progression. In this
way we can gain for ourselves peace and satisfaction and
happiness in this life and have a hope of eternal life in the
world to come." (*Conference Reports*, October 1959, p. 51.)

Marion G. Romney

"I feel certain that if, in our homes, parents will read
from the Book of Mormon prayerfully and regularly, both by
themselves and with their children, the spirit of that great
book will come to permeate our homes and all who dwell
therein. The spirit of reverence will increase; mutual respect
and consideration for each other will grow. The spirit of

contention will depart. Parents will counsel their children in greater love and wisdom. Children will be more responsive and submissive to the counsel of their parents. Righteousness will increase. Faith, hope, and charity—the pure love of Christ—will abound in our homes and lives, bringing in their wake peace, joy, and happiness." (*Conference Reports*, April 1980, p. 90.)

Boyd K. Packer
"If your students are acquainted with revelations, there is no question—personal or social or political or occupational—that need go unanswered. Therein is contained the fulness of the everlasting gospel. Therein we find principles of truth that will resolve every confusion and every problem and every dilemma that will face the human family or any individual in it." ("Teach the Scriptures," an address to religious educators, October 14, 1977, p. 5.)

Second Timothy 3:15-17
"That from a child thou hast known the holy scriptures, which are able to make thee wise unto salvation through faith which is in Christ Jesus.

"All scripture is given by inspiration of God, and is profitable for doctrine, for reproof, for correction, for instruction in righteousness: that the man of God may be perfect, throughly furnished unto all good works."

First Nephi 15:24
"I said unto them that it was the word of God; and whoso would hearken unto the word of God, and would hold fast unto it, they would never perish; neither could the temptations and the fiery darts of the adversary overpower them unto blindness, to lead them away to destruction."

Second Nephi 32:3
"Angels speak by the power of the Holy Ghost; where-

fore, they speak the words of Christ. Wherefore, I said unto you, feast upon the words of Christ; for behold, the words of Christ will tell you all things what ye should do."

Jacob 2:8

"It supposeth me that they have come up hither to hear the pleasing word of God, yea, the word which healeth the wounded soul."

Alma 31:5

"Now, as the preaching of the word had a great tendency to lead the people to do that which was just—yea, it had had more powerful effect upon the minds of the people than the sword, or anything else, which had happened unto them— therefore Alma thought it was expedient that they should try the virtue of the word of God."

Helaman 3:29-30

"Yea, we see that whosoever will may lay hold upon the word of God, which is quick and powerful, which shall divide asunder all the cunning and the snares and the wiles of the devil, and lead the man of Christ in a strait and narrow course across that everlasting gulf of misery which is prepared to engulf the wicked—and land their souls, yea, their immortal souls, at the right hand of God in the Kingdom of heaven, to sit down with Abraham, and Isaac, and with Jacob, and with all our holy fathers, to go no more out."

II. The following quotes help identify the necessity of time and effort in scripture study.

Spencer W. Kimball

"One cannot become a 'doer of the word' without first becoming a 'hearer.' And to become a 'hearer' is not simply to stand idly by and wait for chance bits of information; it is to seek out and study and pray and comprehend." ("How Rare a Possession—the Scriptures!" *Ensign*, September 1976, p. 2.)

Harold B. Lee

"Are you brethren continually increasing your testimony by diligent study of the scriptures? Do you have a daily habit of reading the scriptures? If we're not reading the scriptures daily, our testimonies are growing thinner, our spirituality isn't increasing in depth." (Address at a Regional Representatives seminar, December 12, 1970, p. 10.)

Howard W. Hunter

"Those who delve into the scriptural library, however, find that to understand requires more than casual reading or perusal—there must be concentrated study. It is certain that one who studies the scriptures every day accomplishes far more than one who devotes considerable time one day and then lets days go by before continuing. Not only should we study each day, but there should be a regular time set aside when we can concentrate without interference." ("Reading the Scriptures," *Ensign*, November 1979, p. 64.)

Notes

Chapter One: Why Study the Scriptures?

1. James M. Paramore, Scripture Motivation lesson outline, lesson 4, p. 9.
2. Rafael A. Galindez, "What Daily Scriptural Study Has Meant to Me," *Ensign*, December 1972, p.22.
3. Dean Jarman, *New Era*, November 1973, p. 30.

Chapter Two: Not Read, but Search!

1. Robert B. Day, *They Made Mormon History* (Salt Lake City: Deseret Book Company, 1968), pp. 125-26.

Chapter Three: Recognizing and Fulfilling Our Spiritual Hunger

1. Spencer W. Kimball, "When the World Will Be Converted," address given at a Regional Representative seminar, April 4, 1974.
2. Molly H. Sorensen, "How Does One Learn to Be a Good Mother?" *Ensign*, April 1977, p. 33.
3. Boyd K. Packer, address delivered to stake presidents and Regional Representatives, April 1982, p. 2.
4. Parley P. Pratt, *Autobiography of Parley Parker Pratt* (Salt Lake City: Deseret Book Company, 1938), p. 37.
5. Howard W. Hunter, "Reading the Scriptures," *Ensign*, November 1979, p. 64.

Chapter Four: Hearing the Voice of the Lord

1. S. Dilworth Young, "Know That I Am!" *Improvement Era*, April 1969, p. 49.
2. Paul Sheldon, "I Was Expecting to Prove or Disprove the Church Intellectually," *Ensign*, December 1972, p. 33.
3. Marion G. Romney, "Records of Great Worth," *Ensign*, September 1980, p. 4.
4. Barbara Bartocci, *Readers Digest*, March 1984, pp. 14-16.

Chapter Five: Learning a New Language, the Language of the Scriptures

1. Joseph Fielding Smith, *Answers to Gospel Questions,* vol. 2 (Salt Lake City: Deseret Book Company, 1958), p. 17.
2. William James Mortimer, "The Coming Forth of the LDS Editions of Scripture," *Ensign,* August 1983, p. 41.
3. Bruce R. McConkie, *The Mortal Messiah,* vol. 1 (Salt Lake City: Deseret Book Company, 1979), p. 317.
4. Ibid., p. 334.
5. Ibid., p. 358.
6. Dorothy Kaye Wallace, "I Never Did Find Reading Very Exciting," *Ensign,* December 1972, p. 32.

Chapter Six: Satan's Price Switch

1. James E. Talmage, *Jesus the Christ,* (Salt Lake City: Deseret Book Company, 1973), p. 247.

Chapter Seven: Family Scripture Study

1. Dean L. Larsen, address given at a Regional Representatives seminar, April 1, 1983.
2. Belle S. Spafford, *Women in Today's World,* (Salt Lake City: Deseret Book Company, 1971), pp. 43-44.

Chapter Eight: Blessing the Lives of Others

1. Sterling W. Sill, "The Three I's," *New Era,* August 1979, pp. 4-5.
2. LeGrand Richards, *LeGrand Richards Speaks* (Salt Lake City: Deseret Book Company, 1972), p. 142.
3. Bruce R. McConkie, address given at a Regional Representatives seminar, April 2, 1982, pp. 1-2.
4. Boyd K. Packer, "Principles," *Ensign,* March 1985, p. 9.

Index